A Beggar at the Door

A Beggar at the Door

Longer and Shorter Psalms

Josh Goldberg

Foreword by
Beth Benedix

Albion
Andalus

Boulder, Colorado

2015

"The old shall be renewed,
and the new shall be made holy."
— Rabbi Avraham Yitzhak Kook

Albion-Andalus Inc.
P. O. Box 19852
Boulder, CO 80308
www.albionandalus.com

Design and composition by Albion-Andalus Inc.

Cover design by Sari Wisenthal-Shore.

Cover image of the acrylic painting, "Yud, or the Last Night" by Josh Goldberg (www.joshgoldbergtucson.com). Private collection, used with permission.
Illustrations by Josh Goldberg. All photos by Steve Torregrossa.

Manufactured in the United States of America

ISBN-13: 978-0692403877 (Albion-Andalus Books)
ISBN-10: 0692403876

To my higher powers:

wife Anita, daughters Aleysha and Alia,
granddaughter Avery.

CONTENTS

ACKNOWLEDGMENTS

FOR THEIR ENCOURAGEMENT and support of the creative process, I wish to deeply thank the following souls: my family for their continuous love and support, Beth Benedix for graciously agreeing to write the forward, study partners Rabbi Stephanie Aaron and Lisa Mishler who listened, editor and publisher Netanel Miles-Yépez for his expertise, and students at The Drawing Studio who inspire me to be a better teacher and painter. It is their book as much as it is mine.

— J.G.

PREFACE

ONE CAN FIND the lore of beggars in Hinduism, Buddhism and Zen, Sufism, Daoism, the poetic traditions of China and Japan. These unsettling characters are on the outskirts of conventional living: society's exiles tangled in tatters, coming out of side streets and back alleys. Or in the rearview mirror of our speeding car, we sometimes sight the occasional beggar saint, sage, or seer under a freeway, moving in slow motion from shadow to shaft of sun, tapping off a cigar ash in a concrete corner of oblivion. As a Jewish expression I sit beside them weeping and singing psalms along the dark road of Cosmic Exile.

— Josh Goldberg
Tucson, Arizona, 2015

FOREWORD

"ONLY IN THIS WAY can writing be done," Kafka exhales into his diary, the afterglow of one long stretch of evening, sky now returning to light, that gave birth to his story, "The Judgment." "Only with such coherence, with such complete opening out of the body and soul... the always clear eyes." So, too, Josh Goldberg's psalms plunge into clarity, coherence. Each is an opening-out, lamentation and embrace, exquisite, raw, complete. The light that animates his swirling, sprawling canvases is distilled here, pulsing with immediacy, tempered and radiant.

Like the psalms of tradition, Josh's psalms are blessing, praise, prayer and plea. These are psalms that disclose, disrobe, disrupt; the veil is by turns coaxed open and ripped aside, in gestures by turns gentle and brutal. "Master of Breath" is entreated to sanctify the moment, for instance, "when glow of the sun / beneath the eyelid / compliments the smile / on the face of the severed head." But the fall into time is also the finding of home, of transparency: "before coming into the world / we loll as orphan souls... / before entering / our bodies as rain mist / we stow away on fleets." The world disclosed, disrobed, disrupted is menacing in its sharpness: "those who slander / are lovers of havoc / their throats an open grave / where insects flourish / to lay their eggs." This is who we are, we lovers of havoc, we courters of ego. But, so, too, the lifted veil offers the possibility for wisdom-bringing awareness, that fragile comfort: "There are no questions / only answers /

slender thoughts written in ice / on the windows of the soul / as hair on the arms of the wise."

These are psalms marked deeply by their mystical turn: part passionate frenzy, love-drunk rapture, part hushed whisper, a secret passed from lover to Beloved. These are psalms of promise, supplication, surrender. Naked, they present themselves, beggar at the door, lover in the making: "I ask myself / from God what do you want / great fluttering eyelashes / handshake, lover's kiss?" Exhausted here, exasperated by the weight of silence, the burden of unvoiced wishes perhaps fickle, disarming, malicious. After all, we are told, "The Lord walks / His thief walk / kisses growing dark on His lips / stealing lives / in silent litany." Sometimes this scorned lover's accusation turns inward, and, in these moments, it seems what matters most is acknowledging, simply, that we suffer— from separation and isolation, from "abandoned words" and "lifeless sentences," from missed opportunity and ignorance, from the "beautiful neglected awakenings of divine love." From the illusion of ego that squanders our chances to see and seek the world hidden in the world: "I am my body / I am my thoughts / I am myself."

Still there is tenderness, intimacy. Heart-salving domesticity that is *tikkun olam:* "Oh to make love on a soft bed / without stones, shards of glass / the thousand images of myself / scattered in disunion / beyond the rush of time / just my soul washed / like a dish in a sink / scoured clean / left to dry by the window / complete in the morning light." And, still, these psalms announce a directive for the soul-scoured-clean: "We are given a self / an egg within the body... / to remember the forgotten sound / God's long sigh / so we can say, *hineni,* I am here / in breaking dawn." To say and to remember: *I am here.* Rilke smiles, sensing here a kindred: he of all poets recognizes this imperative to speak into being, to speak into memory, the material remnants, the blink of an eye. Josh's psalms assure us we are seen, we "invalids," "splendor upon splendor," "lightly whispered / as a cyphered hymn / laden with possibilities." His psalms crack through the heart, shimmer, iridescent, "beyond anything that can be said."

— Beth Benedix, Associate Professor of Religious Studies and Literature, DePauw University

LONGER PSALMS

Within me a desert
burnt stones, barren sands

razor winds angled, cutting
a great wall like the one in China

long ago irrigated fields
spent spring water lakes

sunken corridors deep within
clawing crooked descent

to the slum surfaces in a city of dust
to write God's great name

Last of the line
last of the name

this drop from Adam
opens his mouth
in the center of the storm

In solitude
hat clutched
over His heart

God stirs the dead
awakening

Master of Breath:

Bless the moment
when glow of the sun

beneath the eyelid
compliments the smile
on the face of the severed head

Bless the horizon
first light laden

with warm bees
hanging as a curtain
from chilled lips

I am an invalid who burns
deep in the abyss of pain

unbreak my heart
do not close
but disclose me

my Lord God
return my eyes
to hollow sockets

flush out fires of my heart
from sewer pipes of snow

Oh to make love on a soft bed
without stones, shards of glass

the thousand images of myself
scattered in disunion

beyond the rush of time
just my soul washed

like a dish in a sink
scoured clean

left to dry by the window
complete in the morning light

It is said voices of birds
contain mysteries of Torah

unlike the image of the dog
legs up at twilight
dead stiff in prayer

You who cooled Abraham's kiln
remember my blistering

I now stand before You
hollow, shaken out
mercy be upon me

Let Your balm
caress our being

our time runs out
a panicked horse
from a burning barn

faith without wisdom, nothing
pity us planted in the soil of ignorance

beside sleeping waters
counting ninety-nine
names of suffering

I ask myself
from God what do *you* want

great fluttering eyelashes
handshake, lover's kiss?

don't think – be quick
sorrow will steal your heart

the soul speaks only of love
count tears not sins

of my ravished heart
if I am to be a true lover

The world is a dream
foam thrown up

by a Great Wave
filled with the pain of separation

And I – I am on my way
drunk, ruined, burnt

hand in hand with the Beloved
to skinny-dip in the Ocean

I tell myself
don't get caught

in the illusion
I am my body

I am my thoughts
I am my self

don't get caught
in any deception

foot-bound
broken-winged

We are given a self
an egg within the body

to know the difference between yolk and shell
find the world hidden in the world

learn the ache of isolation
beyond the subterrane

to remember the forgotten sound
God's long sigh

so we can say, *hineni*, I am here
in breaking dawn

Before coming into the world
we loll as orphan souls

on the shore of listening.
With the sound of the Ocean

before secretly entering
our bodies as rain mist

we stow away on fleets
roving schooners

intimately taking on water
as we sleep inside deep spaces

You who are born will be buried
say you know the heart of God

show me everything as is
not what appears to be

speak to me of fire
not smoke

whisper in each ear about light
when I see only shadow

say His name
as you look at my face

An Ocean under my skin
where I swim long salty strokes

sink in ecstasy at noon
rise sober at midnight

an Ocean drop by drop
in every one of us

daylight on the left
night on the right

where we study, pray, and speak
beyond anything that can be said

Beloved spreads a bedroll
beneath the space of His tongue

drops a grist of darkness
- a grain of sand in an oyster -

infinitesimal, unsplittable
a tittle of divine completeness

irritable God-bit
against shapeless walls of the soul

to lick, star-clustered,
into iridescent mother-of-pearl

Where do they go
abandoned words, lifeless sentences

torn angry sketches tossed to the floor
incomplete thoughts, misremembered names

dropped hints, flat notions
the painted over areas of fruitless forms

shadows of unacceptance
the ill-fated of our creation?

Resurrected into prayer books for the unborn
fours angels to each disregarded dropping

sweet as a fingertip dipped in honey
one to hold, one to turn, one to read, one to ponder

no longer in need of correction
lake-perfect

beautiful neglected awakenings
of divine love

Rumble of panic behind pain, suffering
fear of dying into ocean nothingness

leaving behind memories of bed sheets in the sun
scent of hawthorn in the rain

cupping my wife's warm breasts
fragments of wondrous conceit

until Night comes sullen round the corner
slipping over my head like a bed sheet

I will put my swelling cortex on hold
- the horrifying as well as the holy -

walk across that dark water
a laughing blind man nowhere to go

SHORTER PSALMS

Pre-Face

Pigeons dark
against winter twilight
in silent minyans
spelling invisible letters
secret prayers

The Lord is my crag and crevice
Him I shall take to
where bristles are thin
let no dust fall on us
nor into emptiness descend

Since Lord I cannot gracefully
slip away from You
I shall remain in the narrow attic of my heart
a beggar at the door
in precious unease

As the Lord seduces
the melting snow
I shall myself uncage
leaving nothing front nor back
but wounds and tongues

Listen well to me:
the bite of the ignorant
the Lord makes sweet
but a wintry heart
your soul He'll break

Lord, hear my prayer:

Be a light to my eyes
a crown to my head
egg-hatched
hold my hand
I gag on the smallest of flies

Grant me Grace:

Lord, my God, You are very great
I am a flea at the foot of a lion
I am a walled city holding fast
let me fall no more
You, O Lord I lift my heart

On His right palm
the Lord sets whirlwinds
on His left
the inchworm
that I am

Responsa:

In the interstices of unreason
the odor of night
cristo viene
stomach churning
smelling of lilac water

Erect this phallic soul
in the kingdom of Love
that I may explode
Hallelujah, Hallelujah
The Lord is Great!

A whore in foul weather
I seek shelter in You
in the rain of winter's grace
during the hour of love
let my tongue take flight

White stones in the night
toward a black-veined horizon
sky of a thousand stars
fills my skull
from which I drink

In my falcon's eye
rivers back-source
mountains down-grow
a hole made in a shell
I sight all You see

There are no questions
only answers
slender thoughts written in ice
on the windows of the soul
as hair on the arms of the wise

Hear my plea:

Grant me grace O Lord
for I stumble
I am a dry field seeking rain
a lost gaze in my own city
fuel me for my fire's meal

I acclaim the Lord
that my ancestors exalted
so their speaking
may be as generous
as my kissing

Those who slander
are lovers of havoc
their throats an open grave
where insects flourish
to lay their eggs

For David and his seed:
We are splendor upon splendor
the seven affections of the heart
cannot contain the abyss of our longing
as we stagger from sunstroke to sunstroke

We are invalids
called with our own voice
by the cut flesh
crackling like paper flowers
over a burning lake

Praised be the Lord
hidden in His essence
pale as the white horse
desire twinkling
in a red eye

We are but a pretext
for His playing all parts
lightly whispered
as a cyphered hymn
laden with possibilities

The Lord walks
His thief walk
kisses growing dark on His lips
stealing lives
in silent litany

Now do I know
the invisible crag of contradiction
the conceit of civilization
when all colors of the spectrum are spun
the eye sees them as white

Drawn down
in greatest concealment
the soul within a body
in divine repose
as beryl in amethyst

He sees

- when the body sleeps
                    the soul enfolding like a fetus
- an old leg bone
- a wall, a house with no windows
- falling evening

- a woman so close there's no trace of
  her existence
    - the heart of my father
                    as he sits in the Dying Chair
  - a child on tip toes

Index of First Lines

LIST OF ILLUSTRATIONS

"The Gatekeeper." 26.5in. x 40in. Charcoal and ink on paper. Page 2.

"Scene from a Receding Past." 18in. x 14in. Ink on paper. Page 6.

"The Face Has But One Star." 29.75in. x 41.5in. Charcoal on paper. Page 14.

"Each Time Night Unbolts Your Door." 26.6in. x 40in. Charcoal on paper. Page 24.

"Burnt Book (Torah of the Void)." 22.5in. x 30in. Charcoal on paper. Page 32 (should be viewed horizontally).

"Blindsight." 26.5in. x 40in. Charcoal, ink, and water on paper. Page 42. (should be viewed horizontally).

JOSH GOLDBERG is a poet, translator, essayist, book critic, and visual artist. Having studied studio art, art history, and Japanese language and literature at Michigan State University, California State University, UCLA, and the University of Arizona, Goldberg teaches Advanced Abstract Painting at The Drawing Studio in Tucson, Arizona. His artwork can be seen at Davis Dominguez Gallery in Tucson, Susan Street Fine Art in Solana Beach, California, and joshgoldbergtucson. com.

Made in the USA
San Bernardino, CA
13 May 2015